SCOOP AND HUDSON

AND THE

DEADLY GERM

TONY WILKINSON

WALKER BOOKS
AND SUBSIDIARIES
LONDON • BOSTON • SYDNEY

A **NEWS CONTEST** FOR KIDS! FIRST PRIZE, YOU GET TO WRITE FOR A BIG CITY NEWSPAPER! WOW! THANKS A LOT, MR PETERSEN!

LOOK AT ME! A HOT-SHOT **INTERNATIONAL REPORTER**. I SHOULD BE WRITING THE NEWS, NOT DELIVERING IT!

HEY, SCOOP! SEEN THIS?

WHERE CAN I FIND A BIG STORY IN A SMALL TOWN LIKE LITTLE LAKE?

LATER

HI, MR BROCCOLI! ANY WORLD EXCLUSIVE STORIES FOR ME TODAY?

69¢ /lb

SURE, SIGNOR SCOOP! THE PRICE OF LETTUCE IS UP AGAIN!

NO FOOLING?

THIRD RISE THIS MONTH!

RULE ONE OF BIG-SHOT REPORTING – VEGETABLES AREN'T NEWS, OK?

RATS! NOTHING INTERESTING EVER HAPPENS AROUND HERE!

OWWW!

THIS WAY UP

SEE? THAT OLD BOX HAS MORE LIFE THAN MOST FOLKS IN LITTLE LAKE...

WAIT A MINUTE – BOXES DON'T **HOWL**! DO THEY?

HOLD THE FRONT PAGE! A **DOG** IN A BOWLER HAT!

HUDSON – **BUTLER**, CANINE DIVISION, TO BE PRECISE, SIR.

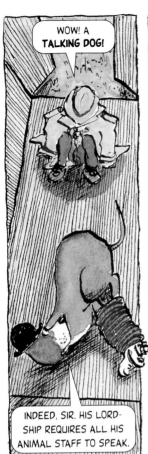

WOW! A **TALKING DOG!**

INDEED, SIR. HIS LORD-SHIP REQUIRES ALL HIS ANIMAL STAFF TO SPEAK.

LORDSHIP? WHAT LORDSHIP?

LORD CHILBLANE OF CHILBLANE CASTLE, SIR.

IF YOU WOULD BE SO KIND AS TO UNTIE THESE ROPES, SIR, I SHALL EXPLAIN.

CHILBLANE CASTLE, BEHIND US, SIR, IS ONE OF THE FINEST IN SCOTLAND!

HUH?

SCOTLAND? CASTLE? HOLD IT RIGHT THERE! THIS IS NOT SCOTLAND, HUDSON, IT'S THE **USA**. THE PRAIRIES! OK?

USA?

AND THAT "CASTLE" IS A GRAIN ELEVATOR!

OH, DEAR, SIR, MY HEAD! IT'S ALL COMING BACK TO ME!

HIS LORDSHIP WAS ON A FUNDRAISING TOUR OF AMERICA TO RESTORE THE CASTLE. . .

I OVERHEARD HIS LORDSHIP TALKING TO A SINISTER BUSINESSMAN. . .

THEN **TWO SCOUNDRELS** DRAGGED ME INTO THE BUSHES AND KNOCKED ME OUT!

I AWOKE TO FIND MYSELF IN A BOX. . .

I COULD HEAR THE SOUND OF A TRAIN. THEN I FELT MYSELF FALLING. . .

THIS WAY UP

I AM AFRAID THAT IS THE LAST THING I CAN REMEMBER, SIR.

WHAT A STORY! A TALKING DOG, A SCOTTISH LORD, A **KIDNAP**. WOW!

THIS IS BIG ENOUGH TO WIN THE NEWS CONTEST! HUDSON, YOU'RE A GENIUS!

I BEG YOUR PARDON, SIR?

BUT YOU GOT TO KEEP THIS UNDER YOUR HAT, OK? THE OTHER REPORTERS WOULD KILL FOR A STORY LIKE THIS.

OTHER REPORTERS, SIR?

ESPECIALLY THE **TREACLE TWINS**. WHATEVER YOU DO, DON'T SPEAK TO THEM, OK?

BOO!

OH, NO — IT'S THEM! NOT A WORD, REMEMBER!

HI, SCOOP! GREAT PET DOG.

YEAH, WHAT DO YOU CALL HIM?

HIS NAME'S HUDSON. BUT HE'S NOT A PET HE'S A. . .

'COS DADDY DON'T ALLOW NO PETS ON HIS **RENTED PROPERTY**, RIGHT, TRACEY-LEE?

SURE THING, TAMMY-JO. IF HE FOUND SCOOP WITH A PET DOG, HE'D THROW HIM AND HIS MOM RIGHT OUT OF THEIR HOUSE!

EITHER THAT, OR THE DOG WOULD HAVE TO BE **DESTROYED**!

CHAPTER 2

WELCOME TO **BOOKWORM CONTROL**, GENTLEMEN – A UNIVERSE OF KNOWLEDGE AT YOUR FINGERTIPS! YOU ARE SUPERHEROES DESTINED TO SAVE THE PLANET, CORRECT?

NOT EXACTLY, MA'AM. **I'M SCOOP**. I'M IN SIXTH GRADE. AND THIS IS **HUDSON**. HE'S A KIND OF BUTLER . . .

CANINE DIVISION, MA'AM.

NOW, LET'S SEE – "P" FOR PYROMANIACS, POISONERS AND POLLUTERS. YES, THERE HE IS!

WE'VE GOT TO STOP HIM, MISS PARCHMENT! CALL HIM UP, RIGHT NOW!

MR POLLUTION HIMSELF! **LUCIFER GERM**, THE HEAD OF GLOBAL FILTH! HE HAS TAKEN OVER THE ENTIRE COUNTRY OF **N'GOLI** IN AFRICA. HIS FACTORIES ARE KILLING THE RAINFOREST! HE TURNS **POISONOUS WASTE** INTO BUILDING MATERIAL, THEN SELLS IT ALL OVER THE WORLD!

WITH RESPECT, MA'AM, I THINK IT MIGHT BE WISE TO WORK OUT A PLAN BEFORE WE APPROACH MR GERM.

YOU'RE RIGHT, HUDSON!

FOR VILLAINS OF MR GERM'S NOTORIETY, I HAVE ALWAYS RECOMMENDED THE **FLIM-FLAM GAMBIT**.

WE WILL SEND MR GERM AN INVITATION HE CANNOT RESIST!

NEXT DAY

HUDSON, WAKE UP! HE FELL FOR IT! HE'S SENDING HIS **PRIVATE JET** TO TAKE US TO HIS HEADQUARTERS TOMORROW!

DO NOT DISTURB

TOMORROW? GERM'S HEADQUARTERS? GOOD HEAVENS!

LET US HOPE THAT MISS PARCHMENT HAS MADE OUR **SPYING EQUIPMENT** IN TIME!

SPYING EQUIPMENT? WHAT SPYING EQUIPMENT?

YOU WILL SEE, SIR.

I HAVEN'T HAD TIME TO TEST YOUR BOWLER HAT, HUDSON.

WHAT?

BUT THE BOW-TIE IS WORKING ADMIRABLY. . .

HUH?

JUST ONE LITTLE MINUTE! WOULD SOMEONE MIND EXPLAINING WHAT IS GOING ON?

MY APOLOGIES, SIR. YOU SEE, IN ORDER FOR THE **FLIM-FLAM GAMBIT** TO SUCCEED, WE SHALL NEED RECORDED EVIDENCE. . .

AND A **TRANSMITTER SWITCH** IMPLANTED ON THE END OF MY TAIL!

WOW! LUCIFER GERM, HERE WE COME!

A **MOVIE CAMERA** HAS BEEN HIDDEN INSIDE MY NEW BOWLER HAT. . .

A **MICROPHONE** INSIDE MY NEW BOW-TIE. . .

CHAPTER 3

NEXT DAY

LOOK, HUDSON! DOWN THERE – **N'GOLI!**

INDEED, SIR! TIME TO PREPARE THE EQUIPMENT.

ONE MINIATURE MOVIE CAMERA INSIDE THE HAT. . .

CHECK!

ONE BOW-TIE MICROPHONE. . .

TESTING, ONE-TWO-THREE!

ONE TAIL-SWITCH TRANSMITTER. . .

IT'S WORKING!

IT'S HIM! HE'S COME TO MEET US!

WELCOME TO N'GOLI, MY FRIENDS. **LUCIFER GERM**, AT YOUR SERVICE.

SO THIS IS YOUR FAMOUS BOWLER-HATTED DOG, EH?

HIS NAME'S HUDSON, SIR.

FRIENDLY CREATURE, ISN'T HE? LOOK! HE'S WAGGING HIS TAIL!

AND NOW OUR TOUR, MR SCOOP. YOU SHALL SEE THE **GLOBAL FILTH EMPIRE** IN ALL ITS GLORY!

HUDSON, BEHIND US, LOOK! IT CAN'T BE. . .CAN IT?

CHAPTER 4

SURPRISE, SURPRISE!

HI, SCOOP! PLEASED TO SEE US? WE GOT THE ROOM RIGHT NEXT TO YOURS! RIGHT TAMMY-JO?

RIGHT TRACEY-LEE – THE **VIP SUITE!** OUR UNCLE TOMMY TREACLE IS REAL BIG BUDDIES WITH MR GERM!

COME ON IN, GUYS! SCOOP NEEDS YOUR HELP!

'CAUSE WE HEARD **WEIRD NOISES** COMING FROM HIS ROOM!

I DO BELIEVE YOU'RE RIGHT, TRACEY-LEE!

OUT OF THE WAY, SCOOP!

HEY, STOP! YOU CAN'T GO OUT THERE. . .OUCH!

BOOKWORM TO HUDSON. ALL YOUR **SECRET RECORDINGS** SAFELY RECEIVED. JUST ONE QUESTION, HUDSON. . .

YES, MA'AM?

WHO ARE THOSE TWO **HORRIBLE GIRLS** SNEAKING UP BEHIND YOU?

WOW, LOOK AT THIS! SCOOP'S REALLY GONNA BE IN TROUBLE NOW!

GUARDS! GUARDS!

QUICK, HUDSON – LET'S GET OUT OF HERE!

CHAPTER 5

MEANWHILE...

YOU CERTAIN ABOUT THIS, MISS PARCHMENT?

964

YES, OF COURSE!

THE **MARINES** ARE THE ONLY LANGUAGE GERM UNDERSTANDS, CAPTAIN GRIT!

GOOD LUCK.

FORWARD! TO "THE FILTHY GLOBE"!

THERE SHE IS! SLOW DOWN!

AAARGHH! GET THAT DOG OFF ME!!

HELP! MY LEG!

GRRRR!

THAT'S THE **THIRD EXECUTIONER** THAT DOG HAS BITTEN! STAND BACK, I'LL DO THE JOB MYSELF!

COME ON, GERM! IF HUDSON DOESN'T GET YOU, THOSE MARINES WILL!

MARINES? OH, YES, VERY FUNNY, MR SCOOP. AND I SUPPOSE THEY'RE **BEHIND ME** NOW, RIGHT?

BOOM!

RIGHT FIRST TIME, GERM!

CHAPTER 6

FIRST PUBLISHED 1998 BY WALKER BOOKS LTD
87 VAUXHALL WALK, LONDON SE11 5HJ

2 4 6 8 10 9 7 5 3 1

TEXT AND ILLUSTRATIONS
©1998 TONY WILKINSON

THIS BOOK HAS BEEN TYPESET IN
OPTI KARTOON

PRINTED IN SINGAPORE

BRITISH LIBRARY CATALOGUING IN PUBLICATION DATA
A CATALOGUE RECORD FOR THIS BOOK IS AVAILABLE
FROM THE BRITISH LIBRARY.

ISBN 0-7445-4122-0